# SECOND
# NATURE

by Mark Ellis

# Foreword

Almost 20 years ago, on a hot summer's day, I saw from the helicopter I was flying an enticing spot by a lake in a Gloucestershire. The area was clear and so I landed for a sandwich, a swim and a snooze.

A chance lunch with a friend led me to discover that it was for sale, three weeks later I was the proud owner of what is now the Lower Mill Estate.

Nothing was further from my mind than turning the land into, what many now call, one of the world's leading vacation home settlements, an architectural icon and a global standard nature reserve. I just wanted a place in the country for my family amongst nature.

Over the years, as Lower Mill grew on me more and became my home, I began to look at the possibilities of sharing its 550 or so acres with other people and building a limited number of vacation homes that harmonised with nature and people.

What we have quietly developed here still excites me on a daily basis, even all these years on.

It's a beautiful place that hundreds of people now call home. To continue this pride of ownership two of my children, that I brought up here, are today adults running substantial parts of the business.

Mark Ellis has followed the development of Lower Mill for many years. This, his short book, Second Nature, is a glimpse into live at Lower Mill.

If it inspires you to want to return to "Swallows and Amazons" and become part of the Lower Mill community, either by buying a home or occasionally renting one, I think you'll be as happy here as we have always been.

Jeremy Paxton

Founder of Lower Mill.

# 1

## Live to work. Work to live.

This may sound like the kind of thing that part - time Buddhists say without thinking about it much, but it's nonetheless a fundamental truth: we, modern human beings, really don't spend enough time living up to our name and being - as in hanging, chilling, loafing or whatever you call doing not a lot.

We occupy ourselves, for sure. We are effective as what were described by Warren Farrell in his influential 1990 book *Why Men Are The Way They Are* as 'human doings'. We survive, exist, sustain and the rest of it. But somehow just being is seen as wasting time.

It wasn't supposed to be like this in the 21st century. In past decades, we thought we knew perfectly well what this period in history was going to be like. It wasn't that we'd all be wearing one - piece shiny space suits, living in glass bubbles or zipping about in flying cars. Nor was it Stanley Kubrick's famous vision for 2001, of giant spaceships and emotionally unstable computers.

No, the defining characteristic of the 21st century that everyone agreed upon was that work would virtually have disappeared. Sure, we might still put in a couple of hours a week for old time's sake, but the heavy stuff, the pushing and shoving and delivering and farming, would all clearly be done by robots, while the brain strain - the filing, the investment banking, the teaching, the novel writing would obviously be performed by computers.

Indeed, there were grave worries that we wouldn't know what to do with ourselves, that the sheer abundance of leisure hours and the endless opportunity to spend time with our children and families would lead to a global crisis over how to keep ourselves amused.

Amazing new leisure activities, it was concluded, would have to be invented simply to keep us from becoming bored to death. Bizarre pursuits such as playing airborne tennis and even underwater fish racing were suggested as solutions to mankind's leisure problem (and these were the more conservative ideas).

But, instead, the early 21st century is characterised by something nobody imagined; we work harder than ever before. The age of the Web and the BlackBerry, tools designed to lessen the burden of work, have ended up making us busier than ever. Ironically, half of us spend our entire working life slaving long hours tending the very computers that were supposed to make work obsolete.

And so important is work and career that we routinely define ourselves by the peripheral matter of our occupation rather than by our identity as creatures of the natural world - evolved and civilised creatures, but part of the Earth nonetheless.

So, in our 24/7 connected world, we are increasingly uncomfortable with simply 'being'. We're uneasy when unoccupied. We feel that time chilling with our family and friends is wasted, a distraction from the main event of our lives, which is work or, at best, the leisure - themed networking we all do, which seems like fun, but is really just an adjunct to work.

We feel, meanwhile, that pure leisure, hanging out in the natural landscape - or, yes, lazing at home, on the sofa, listening to music or watching movies or even snoozing in a hammock - in short, time spent doing stuff for no real purpose other than fun and relaxation, is unproductive, un - educational, uncompetitive, unhealthy and unworthy of our status as professional, educated 21st- century humans.

Neglecting our children (along with rare, concentrated bursts of smothering and over - indulging them out of the guilt caused by the neglect) is a concomitant of this craven workaholic lifestyle. Some of these kids may become out - and - out sociopaths. Most will see the less obviously, growing up into the more socially acceptable form of delinquent one who merely works too hard and neglects his kids just as his parents neglected him.

Of course, we all know intuitively that life shouldn't be like this. We are aware, if only at the deepest, cellular level, that regularly enjoying real leisure is no less than the secret of life - that relaxation, idling, gossiping, playing, socialising (as opposed to networking), learning (at least in a non - structured, passive sense), interacting with nature, and (most essentially) being part of both a family and a living, vibrant, meaningful community, are as key to a physically and mentally healthy life as breathing.

In his highly regarded book, *The Joy of Laziness: How to Slow Down and Live Longer*, German scientist Professor Peter Axt has gone so far as to argue that idling about for a significant part of your time is the key to a long life and the antidote to professional stress.

'The benefits of procrastination are grossly undervalued in modern society,' says this wise researcher. 'People are working longer hours and trying to fit more into every day. We always think we have to be achieving something, but just vegetating for at least half your free time could be more healthy.'

And while we're feeling uncomfortable about the way 99 per cent of us conduct our lives for 90 per cent of the time, here's another point for today's busy professionals to ponder.

Think of your ten best friends, your real soulmates, not just colleagues. Now calculate how much time you expect to spend in total with each of them between now and when you retire. (Emailing and chatting on social networking sites doesn't count for this exercise.)

So does the total amount of time you are ever going to spend with your dearest friends and buddies add up to a couple of days? A week or two? It would be surprising if it were more. For not only does our unexpectedly busy 21stcentury lifestyle preclude much quality time with children, parents and family, it also reduces interaction with friends to as little a brief dinner date keyed into an electronic diary every year or so.

Ah, you say, but what about holidays? Aren't vacations the salvation we all need to fill with glorious, thoughtful idleness the gaping black hole drilled in our souls by the modern world? In theory, that might be the case. But, as

# The Four Seasons at Lower Mill.

Autumn.

Winter.

Spring.

Summer.

Somerford Villa by Richard Reid. Image by Mark Fairhurst straight from the lens.

we learn more and more as we get older and raise families, holidays are also massively stressful.

Have we been sure to choose the best resort in the best destination? Have we paid the best price? Have we got the best room? Are we eating in the correct, recommended restaurants and ordering the best dishes? Have we ticked off the must - see local sights on the list in the guide book? Most of us who have organised a fair few holidays, especially vacations for the whole family, will be able to list a hundred different, angst - inducing questions of a similar nature.

Middle class professionals who have tired of the all - round lack of 'holiday' afforded by regular holidays usually alight at some point on the vacation home as a solution to the ever more consuming problem of how to carve out a bit of truly satisfying R & R, where there's more by way of blackberry picking than BlackBerry texting.

But the classic home - in - the - country solution to the family holiday conundrum equally has so many drawbacks that a substantial proportion of people abandon the experiment after a while and retreat to the cities, somewhat scorched by the rural experience. Much the same happens to people who buy holiday homes abroad, plus in their case the increasing hassle and expense of flying further diminishes the pleasure.

The worst problem traditional second homers encounter is the sense that the real, working locals resent their relaxed, laid - back presence. The very kind of tranquil mode we try, if we are wise, to adopt in the country, is an affront to working countrymen and women. Paradoxically, it's also the case that the sight of urbanites making money simply by pinging off a few emails from their PDA whilst they are in the queue at the village Post Office could also be seen as practically a form of passive aggression.

Rural people's disquiet at the presence of incomers is not unfounded, either; many 'chocolate box' villages have been transformed into ghost settlements by part time urbanites and local economies nastily warped. In many parts of the UK countryside, average house prices have soared to 20 or more times the local average annual wage. It's a thoroughly unsustainable distortion, and one unlikely to be dented by even the severest cyclical dip in property values.

The change in the demographic of the most desirable rural honeypots means that the people who maintain the delights of villages - the friendly pub, the village store, the agriculture and so on - can no longer afford to live in them.

Widespread broadband access, furthermore, has brought an additional blight on villages - the semi - permanent urban worker, who spends incrementally more and more of his or her time holed up in a country home working remotely.

But warping the British village's demographic and the uneasy guilt that even the most considerate city dwellers feel about this issue when they move part time to the country are only two of the reasons that the village second home option looks increasingly unattractive.

Many villages that appear peaceful on postcards in reality roar and shake with traffic and other mechanical noise. The average suburban close is a haven of tranquillity by comparison. You bought the country house thinking the worst that could happen was being woken early each morning by the dawn chorus with rooster accompaniment. You end up with your head under the pillow trying to keep out the racket of container trucks and agricultural machinery.

Then there's the maintenance nightmare. The 17th- century listed village house that looked so appealing in Country Life can become a massive, life - sapping headache when you are responsible for preserving its ancient charms and keeping its historic integrity intact - whilst at the same time ensuring that the heating works and the roof keeps out the rain.

Reliance on sometimes unreliable or even truculent local

staff to keep your garden tidy and your house secure can similarly be a trial. The often poor quality of local food supplies encourages second homers to ship in groceries from the big city - and thus magnify local resentment by not patronising the village store for anything other than the odd tin of beans and bundle of kindling.

For a second homer in a village that is split between locals and outsiders, the feeling of isolation can be intense and your only human contact with fellow interlopers - or friends visiting from the city. Should you even wish it, it is unlikely that you as a second home owner will ever quite graduate to feeling like an extra in *The Vicar of Dibley*.

Practically as disturbing as all of the above, however, is something that nobody quite expects when they buy a second home in the country. It's the sense you frequently get in a village that you are some considerable way from being surrounded by nature.

The countryside may be a place of beauty, but it's also a vast factory and somewhere people need to live and do the normal, often quite industrial, things that need doing. Accordingly, fields are mostly private and frequently soaked in agrochemicals. Village streets (the ones away from the thundering trunk road, at least) may be quiet - ish, but are rarely safe enough for kids to play on unsupervised.

And as for the endless rural walks you envisioned when the idea of a country house first came up, they're unlikely to be easy to do without at least getting in the car first to reach the kind of designated area marked by those pernicious white - on - brown signs as an officially countrified destination. Some rural idyll. No wonder the expression 'staycation' - spending holidays in your own back garden - has so mushroomed in our consciousness in recent years.

It was to address these very issues - the importance in our stressed modern lives of taking time to chill out, the urgent need to promote family - based activities, the hope of connecting urban people with the countryside and good design - that Jeremy Paxton founded Lower Mill in the early 1990s.

He has since quietly grown it into the phenomenon it is today - a unique vacation living location in the Cotswolds, founded on principles of harmonising man, wildlife and ecology in a sustainable, architecturally exciting environment built for the long term - by which Paxton means hundreds, possibly a thousand or more, years.

Paxton didn't have a clear idea when he acquired the land of the way it is today or the way it will be tomorrow. A self - confessed 'partially reformed beach bum' who had just sold a successful magazine business, he bought the then 550 acres after landing his helicopter there because he fancied a snooze and a swim in one of the string of seven or so lakes.

'I never had a grand plan,' says Paxton. 'I bought it because I'm a country boy by upbringing but had been living among the bright lights of the city for some time, and it seemed like a great place to hang out. Even now, the plan is fluid and organic in its emergence as I have deliberately gone for slow growth so I can keep learning lessons along the way and making it a process of my ongoing imagination.'

'So I lived in the farmhouse there for about three years and just spent the time hanging out, driving the tractor, cutting the grass and evolving what I wanted to do as the next stage. I knew for sure that I wanted to combine nature, people and architecture. But I had to start somewhere and I never had a firm business plan.'

He admits, however, that the idea of creating what he describes as the world's first residential nature reserve formed in his mind early on in the project. The concept of living at weekends and leisure time on a country estate in England was something that the Romans pioneered a while ago. Lower Mill, part of which was Roman settlement, was to take this concept into the 21st and 22nd centuries.

Mark Borkowski and Jeremy Paxton chatting at the reintroduction of the beavers to Lower Mill.

Kevin and Xani McCloud with estate owner Jeremy Paxton reviewing Britain's best small buildin

The glorious Cotswolds - a collection of lakes twice the size of the Norfolk Broads.

zia crew at the Lower Mill's Spa and Country Club.

p fire stories at Lower Mill.

Wildlife conservation was not just at the heart of the project's conception - indirectly, it was the stimulus for Lower Mill happening at all in the form that it has. Living at the farmhouse with his family, Paxton began to pay more attention to the natural environment around him than he had since he was a boy growing up in the country. In particular, he became intrigued by how close it was possible to live to in - the - raw nature without apparently disrupting it.

'I happened to speak to an environmental scientist friend who was telling me how the thing that excited him at the time was the concept of wildlife flourishing because of human contact and not in spite of it. His argument was that if nature is allowed her course unmanaged, she will ultimately strangle an ecosystem because we just don't have the diversity of species that we once had.'

One of the keynote species missing from our ecosystem, the scientist explained, is the beaver, because of the way it prevents overgrowth. Paxton was then introduced to another environmentalist whose doctorate was in what is known as 'disturbance zone modelling'. He had developed computer models to calculate the distance at which humans, especially when accompanied by dogs, which are the most disruptive species in the countryside, become invisible to specific species.

'The modelling comes in useful if, say, you want to create a bat habitat and to know how close people can trample before it disturbs them. And he moved on to Lower Mill and carried out what became a two - year science project working out all these disturbance zones for over 3,500 species. It was a huge amount of modelling, because the disturbance to a lesser emperor dragonfly, for example, is very different and of a very different nature from the disturbance to, say, an otter or a bat.

'English Nature heard about these disturbance zone models and asked to see us and requested my approval to adopt them nationally. They told me that they had been looking for years to find a commercial project that harmonises people, ecology and buildings. And that was what partly led to me developing the concept for Lower Mill as it now is.'

It followed, then, that from the outset, Lower Mill was going to be developed along ethical lines, recognising, for instance, that it is hugely wasteful to spend what would amount to over £40m on a private 550 - acre spread in Gloucestershire with a private spa, a nature reserve and all the pursuits associated with weekending in the country - for just one family. So the founding, defining principle of Lower Mill was from the outset to give up to 600 families the opportunity to own their own, communal country estate with world - class facilities.

Paxton started to develop the more traditionally designed part of the estate, Mill Village, in the mid 1990s. By now, the manmade lakes that distinguish the whole area in which Lower Mill is set were themselves coalescing into a recognised holiday area. It's not common knowledge even in Gloucestershire, but the Cotswold Water Park, as it was by then known, is the largest area of inland water in the UK - bigger than the Norfolk Broads or even the Lake District.

Like a 'real' village (which Lower Mill is today beginning to resemble, with its variety of distinct areas, each with its own character), Paxton has eased the project through a number of phases. Customary though it is to say that such an undertaking has 'grown organically', it is a little inaccurate in Lower Mill's case. Left to her own devices, Mother Nature doesn't always get it right; sometimes, she needs the help of God's own heavy earthmoving equipment.

So, leaving aside the brilliant modern architecture for which the estate has become world renowned, and notwithstanding that the land itself is of organic quality, having never in its history been sullied by industrial chemicals, the unseen work that has been done over more than a decade of tending, husbanding, draining and otherwise pampering these cherished 550 acres of Gloucestershire is on an epic scale and has cost several millions.

So what is Lower Mill today? In the media, it is variously described as a residential nature reserve, a designer vacation village and even a celebrity resort - the latter, while being not wholly untrue, going only a minuscule fraction of the way towards explaining this genuinely ground - breaking rural living phenomenon.

As with its polymath founder, Lower Mill is a lot of things. Essentially, it is a stretch of meadow, forest and lakeland untouched in decades and subsequently encouraged and nurtured over many years to develop as a nature reserve, ecology project and sustainability experiment of true global significance.

At the same time, a few relatively small parts of the land have been developed into one of the pre - eminent vacation villages in the world. It isn't just one of the world's leading showcases of modernist architecture in a rural setting. Lower Mill has also developed into an extraordinary human community that is attracting growing attention globally - a community of largely middle - class, professional urban families, all seeking broadly the same core values of a healthy, sociable, eco - friendly holiday and weekend home. It makes full use of the joys of the countryside and allows for extended quality time with family and friends, whilst entirely avoiding the kind of disruption to the existing local demographic that concentrations of second homes typically cause.

Lower Mill is also a giant playground offering residents, holiday letters and their families, the extraordinary prospect - unavailable even to the vast majority of people who live permanently in the country - of the run of most of 550 acres of safe, virgin rural landscape and water, along with a world - class spa that on its own would be an attraction worthy of moving to the estate for.

And that's not all. The beginnings of what might be seen as a gigantic art project can be discerned at Lower Mill. Not only does the estate concentrate some of the world's foremost modernist architecture, but it also shows ambitions over the coming years to promote innovative work across many other arts fields. Paxton's Landmark Houses Programme, which was launched at the V & A, is widely regarded as having introduced modernism into the rural landscape.

Nor does Lower Mill shows any sign of being a fleeting phenomenon. While the estate is run by a private company, its vision and ambition is more similar to that of a foundation's. Paxton has gone to and beyond the kind of lengths normally reserved for the great aristocratic landowning families to ensure that Lower Mill remains a family business down the generations, operating the same quality and standards, the same essential pride of ownership ethic, decades and centuries into the future. The succession is already planned, with the next generation of Paxtons already in place working on the estate running substantial parts of the business, having learned the ways of the business and the Lower Mill community from the ground up.

'We view the whole thing as like a giant endowment,' Paxton explains. 'If you take the Duke of Westminster's lease model, which I looked at originally, in which he's got thousand - year leases where you have to pay so much each year to keep your street or square maintained, what I've done is taken it a stage further in sustainability. I've ensured that the ecological model is sustainable for a thousand years. You can't think in three - year horizons with a project of this scope. You have to have a thousand - year business model.'

'It's been a wonderful exercise for the past 12 years harmonising people, ecology and architecture. But for me, the moment I knew it was working was when my son announced many years ago when he was small that he wanted to take the money he'd saved for his new Xbox and spend it instead on fishing equipment. *That* is what this is about. Ultimately, this place actually helps you to be a better parent.'

# 2

'The core of Lower Mill,' as Jeremy Paxton explains, 'is wonderful architecture connected to nature.'

His words come very much to mind on a scorching July Saturday as Lower Mill ranger Kate Gamez takes a group of residents on a hidden wildlife walk that centres on Pike Corner, one of the least visited parts of the estate and one of two officially designated Sites of Special Scientific Interest.

Gamez's walk is not a one - off special event or a paid - for attraction. It's just typical of the kind of activity that continues quietly on the estate and is available to residents year round. It's all too easy to forget that normal villages simply don't have such things - as it is to miss the irony that Lower Mill is palpably more 'in touch' with nature than a comparable village in the 'real' world; here you are, after all living on an internationally regarded nature reserve.

Pike Corner is the best place on the property to find some

of Lower Mill's more elusive residents, including roe deer, muntjac deer, fox, badger and otter. Its plant life is equally amazing, the 37 - acre meadow having been left to do its own thing since the 1930s and probably a century or longer before that too.

As we walk up to Pike Corner, we are immersed in the kind of summer scene that makes you feel you've time travelled back to an idealised England from about 50 years ago, as portrayed in a Ladybird book. Global warming, gridlock, crime and terror might as well be on another planet.

It's not just the gentleness and beauty of what presents itself to the eye. The soundtrack here is perfection too - no traffic at all, the occasional drone of a distant light aircraft, a gentle warm breeze. You can hear crows, the splashes of landing waterfowl and the swooshes of swans upending on the blue lakes, the low, lazy buzz of blue damselflies.

On the lakes, there are great crested grebes, once almost extinct, doing their party trick - the young chicks riding on their parents' back. Overhead, there's a buzzard circling as if it's radio controlled, and even a hobby, a bird of prey rare enough to excite twitchers - obsessive bird watchers. Hundreds of feet higher, the skylarks are wheeling and hollering seemingly for the sheer heck of it.

Down at ground level, Gamez opens up our eyes to another dimension. She points out nearly 20 species of grass in each square metre of Pike Corner's virgin vegetation. Some plants in the meadow, Gamez explains, are prehistoric and would have been trampled on by dinosaurs.

The natural history of other species in the meadow - things a casual hiker would barely even see - is fascinating and thought - provoking. How, for instance, you find yourself wondering in Gamez's wake, did ragwort ever get invented? Yes, ragwort. It's unremarkable - looking stuff that nonetheless contains enough cyanide to kill a cow, should the animal eat it. Fortunately, most cattle (though not horses or goats) are hardwired to ignore ragwort, but out of all creation, a single species of moth, the cinnabar, loves it.

The moth's caterpillars gorge themselves on ragwort and thus, by becoming fat, juicy, wriggling cyanide capsules, avoid being eaten. It's the ultimate protection but, on the off chance some birds forgets that cinnabar caterpillars could seriously disagree with them, they are also colour coded with the international, cross - species - and for all we know intergalactic - danger colours of black and yellow, in threatening stripes.

Even though Gamez knows Pike Corner so well, this adventure playground for naturalists still holds constant surprises for her. As we are walking, she spots a plant she identifies as field scabious, 'I didn't even know we had that on the estate. *That* is a nice find,' she says partly to herself. For a few moments Gamez seems to be in her own world.

As Gamez is enjoying her find, Lower Mill resident Tom Challenor, a fund manager from 90 minutes away in west London, and enjoying a weekend away from a gruelling, ongoing hedge fund acquisition, is explaining why the estate is such a perfect way of enjoying the countryside. 'I think the thing I like about it here most is that we're not ripping the heart out of a village by only being here at weekends,' he says. Even so, at one point his BlackBerry trills with urgent, work - related incoming email, he rolls his eyes and retires briefly some way back from our group.

As you get to the end of Gamez's walk, vacationing humans - complete with their BlackBerrys - seem like just another interesting species in their architect - designed habitat. And there are plenty of them scattered about the estate, knots of kids, parents and grandparents simply enjoying their own, private 550 acres and doing whatever they like. The thought occurs that this place isn't only the perfect form of countryside for urbanites; it is pretty amazing for country people, too.

The broad - based ecological thrust that so characterises

Lower Mill unsurprisingly has its roots directly in Jeremy Paxton's own life experiences.

'I totally adore the countryside,' he explains, 'because it's where I was brought up, in the New Forest. I spent most of my time as a kid scraping my head open going underneath barbed wire fences and running away from farmers who'd be chasing us off a bit of land because we'd found a great swimming hole there. We'd nick fruit out of orchards, and just have a ball, camping in the woods together, even when we were seven and eight years old, building ourselves dirt cross tracks in the woods for our bikes.'

'I also went out a lot with my granddad, Percy Cook, who was a real countryman. I can still skin a rabbit and I know how to make stinging nettle juice, which is actually disgusting, but is richer in iron than spinach. These days, I get so many ideas, and I don't mean just business ideas, in the countryside. I just dream and dream and I still love hanging out and letting the mind wander.'

With such a personal history, it's easier to understand why Lower Mill is growing up into not just an outstanding place to live a modern, comfortable life, but also one of the world's foremost outdoor laboratories for nature conservation.

'We're already the most significant nature reserve in

The Spa after sunset.

The big unpolluted skies give rise to beautiful sunsets, this one over 'Beaver Lake'.

River Thames Mill Race at Lower Mill.

Europe in private hands, being host to over 13,000 trees and over 3,000 species of wildlife - including the famous beavers,' Paxton says. 'I'd also like in due course to build an indoor laboratory for nature conservation. And on the ecology front, we're building links with Oxford University's Wild Crew, its wildlife conservation research unit, which is like an Amnesty International for animals.'

'I'd like Lower Mill to be seen ultimately as an art project that relates to the combination of buildings, wildlife, ecology and people. Already in that vein, we've developed what we call "species rich landscaping", which encourages plentiful wildlife - perhaps 500 species - in a single garden, thus reconnecting people with the natural environment and making people who live most of their lives in the city naturally inclined to be conservation minded. It's moving conservation on from the pure green lobby and making it second nature for concerned urban people who aren't necessarily activists.'

The extensive variety of nature - based activity at Lower Mill stimulates its founder at a fundamental, personal level just as much as giving many of the world's leading architects scope to extend their imagination.

'Things such as the idea of establishing an organic farm are enormously exciting and we have loads of great plans for the original mill. The equestrian and real food projects excite me. The introduction of the European beaver with the WWF excites me. The otter habitat creation and repopulation project - with the infrared cameras where you'll be able to dial in with a VIP log - in if you are one of the owners, and show your friends what's going on - excites me. Plus I've got another project to reintroduce ospreys.'

The list of nature - friendly measures at Lower Mill is constantly being added to. At the time of writing, the estate has the largest bat project in the UK, one of the largest nesting box projects, more than 20 breeding pairs of nightingales, the most extensive house martin project in the UK, an owl breeding programme, newt ponds, tern rafts, grass snake compost heaps, dragonfly posts, insect refuges (created using willow and bamboo in new building and at ground level), a tree nursery, charcoal manufacturing and firewood harvesting.

'All these things are as important to me as the architecture and the building of homes that are designed to stand for thousands of years - the development for want for a better word. I don't even really see myself as a "developer" in the traditional sense. I'm just someone with an interest in the countryside and an interest in design and wanting the two to work symbiotically.'

It is the beavers, of course, which began breeding in the spring of 2007, that put Lower Mill on the map as an ecology project over and above a vacation village.

'Beavers have been extinct here for 500 years,' Paxton says. 'They'd been hunted largely for the secretion from their anal glands which produce a substance much like aspirin. What clinched it for me was that English Nature had been wanting to do this for years. They're an essential part of the eco - system, which has been sadly missed. And they encourage a lot of new growth. Beavers as a species are what you might call the most influential environmental architects.'

'So it all sat perfectly with the ethic and the scope of what I'm doing at Lower Mill. It was the epitome of nature conservation. It's architectural. It's exciting. And nobody else was doing it.'

'We went to Bavaria and looked at the beavers in their natural habitat. The UK government wanted to put them into quarantine for six months so I rented a farm in Devon, which is a perfect beaver habitat. I hired a vet down there and got the leading beaver expert in the world camping out looking after these eight beavers, four pairs. Meanwhile, we were developing a 60 - acre habitat for them on the estate, 30 acres of woodland and 30 of lake.'

Then, there are Paxton's plans for the human inhabitants of the estate. 'I increasingly see the whole place as a spa for body and mind,' he says. 'Ultimately, I want there to be special places on the estate for quiet contemplation, seven of them, where you can watch wildlife and read a good book. I also see seven places where you can go and practise yoga by the lake. And seven places where you can go and hang out in hammocks and chat.' (The seven, incidentally, is to honour the late Barry Sheen, who was Paxton's best friend - seven was his racing number.)

'I want there to be haylofts where people can hang out and chat and lie on the hay. I want people to work on the organic farm. I'm establishing allotments where you can rent a space and don't have to farm it fully. You'd be able to dip into it for half an hour and take back your vegetables or strawberries in a box. So it's the allotment with none of the aggro. Anybody that thinks at all realises that they need to eat fresh healthy real ingredients. And we'd all love to faff around growing and hoeing. It's a therapy thing. But we're all horribly time poor.'

Sustainability, which has tended in recent years to be more of a slogan than a lifestyle for some of us, is, of course, another key driver at Lower Mill. 'The environment and the move towards a zero waste society are very much at the top of the world's agenda and it's becoming increasingly

Just 1 of over 3000 species at Lower Mill.

Raft building at Lower Mill.

Walk along the river to London and experience a forgotten world as well as a new one.

A Lower Mill beaver kit eating breakfast.

in Boland 'photographer of the
rix' shot this at Lower Mill for
Wallpaper in his son's bedroom.

vells Lake - photo Marienne Deus.

ident otters - one of six.

unacceptable to live life without putting thought into what you're doing and how you do it with a view to being less wasteful,' says Paxton.

'Sustainability is an overused and often misunderstood word. To me, it means "consuming less and conserving more". Sustainability is, indeed, a genuine passion for Paxton - and a baseline for the whole range of Lower Mill's operations. 'Our strong connection with nature's ordering system equally does not mean that in order for buildings to be "green" they need to be fitted with wind turbines, water butts, solar panels and sedum roofs. All of these seem to us to be promulgated largely by developers trying to offset buildings that are inefficient in the first place. They are all too often add - ons that are no more than gestures.'

'My view is that homes need to be built to last a thousand years and more, traditionally constructed, made from everlasting materials and hand built by local craftsmen. This will mean they are truly built to conserve energy through solid walls, windows in the right places, proper foundations, solid wood doors, handmade heavy - gauge roof trusses and an ability to change so they can be adapted by future generations. A place that can evolve over time and be everlasting is my definition of sustainable and, although old fashioned, is actually one of the real eco heroes of our time. Buildings we put up today won't need to be demolished in a few years' time - by machines that create a Yeti - sized carbon footprint - and built again using yet more resource - burning materials, as is the case with timber framed construction.'

'With any development project,' he continues, 'the key starting point is to ask, "How can we save energy in a user friendly way?" This can lead to some simple actions that can, when carried out by a sizeable group of people, make a big difference and add to the very realistic sense that Lower Mill is a place where you can get away from a life of chemicals and pollution.'

'For the last ten years, accordingly, Lower Mill, and its partner building company, Conservation Builders, have been applying an "ethical filter" to all its activities. This has put the project at the vanguard of the current push to be more responsible.'

So what is currently being done to make a difference at Lower Mill? One target here is establishing sustainable living via home - grown organic and best practise vegetable and fruit farming for the wider community, with the hope of having enough surplus produce to supply a Lower Mill restaurant, bakery and cheesery, and possibly selected London restaurants.

Then there's the energy question. Paxton's stated ambition is for the entire estate to be not merely zero energy, but to become a net energy creator. The Lower Mill spa, which regularly features in the high - end media as the ultimate luxury resort feature - its swimming pools were described on the Financial Times' *How To Spend It* website as 'the most exclusive in Britain' - is also a paragon of ecological virtue, its eco pool's water chemical - free, and purified instead the natural way, by plants and ecology. The spa pools are just one, albeit well known, contributor in this area: there are dozens of other key measures in daily practice on the estate, both in the construction and the day - to - day functioning of life at Lower Mill.

All buildings are built from recycled or sustainable materials where possible and all building waste, such as gypsum waste product and waste timber, is recycled. Construction vehicle movements are carefully limited and five trees are planted for every new home built, while water butts can be fitted to new properties for rainwater harvesting.

The houses themselves are designed with conservation in mind at every turn. Extensive glazing allows natural light to flood in and for the sun to heat the building, with, in most homes, skilfully planned cross ventilation through large open spaces and atriums to cool those inside in summer. Argon - filled insulated double - glazing, carefully specified, acts to protect the heat inside in the winter. This gives climate control the natural way without harmful air conditioning units.

All materials are chosen carefully and the estate insists on the use of renewable timber and natural products, such as hemp and sheep's wool insulation. Properties that are rendered have an externally insulated system to envelope them. Healthy paints that are VOC (volatile organic compound) and odour - free are used to improve the wellbeing of residents. Central switching is installed for non - essential appliances left on the notorious standby position - Paxton's Planet Switch has gained wide publicity.

Heating in Lower Mill properties is carefully considered, Paxton explains. 'Using condensing gas boilers aids efficiency, and natural heating systems such as wood burners are installed, some of which are 90 per cent efficient and can heat large spaces easily from renewable timber harvested from the estate. We also fit a simple piece of technology that allows you to control your heating via an internet control panel that's ideal for a second home. You can turn the heating up just before you arrive at the house rather than leaving it on to overrun when you are not there. And each new property comes with an eco manual to assist with the green running of the home.'

There's automatic proximity - sensing lighting and ventilation to bathrooms to prevent lights being left on, and rainwater recycling and harvesting is now installed for homeowners. Outside the home, solar lighting stops the drain on energy of lights left on all night. Waste recycling is made easy by multiple bins in the homes and around the estate. All homes are routinely fitted with A - rated appliances to save energy. Low water - use showerheads are fitted as standard. Sustainable transport such as cycling is encouraged by promotion of nearby facilities, the installation of nearby bike racks and covered cycle parking. And, never forgetting the animal neighbours, Lower Mill houses have, wherever possible, good nesting areas under large eaves and special tiles on the roofs to create the perfect perch for passing bats.

'We believe,' Paxton concludes, 'that having a vacation home at Lower Mill - which means, of course, fewer flights to holidays abroad - not so cool these days, and I say that as a pilot myself - should be a relatively effortless way of making a tangible contribution to saving the planet.'

'We believe very much in relaxation down here but, at the same time, we very specifically don't appeal to lazy people. There's always something going on. We don't really want the "fashionable designer clothes but empty life" set to be attracted here. We have people who want to work on allotments, we have people who want to go fishing with their children, who say, "Come on, let's have a great game of Monopoly," or, "Everyone get their boots on, we're strolling out to the pub, having a good two hour walk and we'll have a Sunday roast and then we'll come back in the afternoon and watch a movie or play cards or do some painting." That's what I want Lower Mill to be about, and that's very much how it's working out.'

# 3

It's New Year's Eve at Lower Mill - a cold, clear, still night. The lights are on in most of the houses round Clearwater Lake, their huge modernist windows reflecting into the pristine water. Many of the homes are hosting New Year parties, and each group of revellers is mirrored in the lake, their images only broken up by the occasional waterfowl movement.

In the distance, beyond the liquid swoosh of the birds landing and taking off, there's the sound of an outdoor party and, a few moments away, Lower Mill's village green is *en fête*. The estate's New Year's Eve party, organised entirely by residents and with Paxton not even needing to be there (he is skiing in Switzerland), is a hoot - like a nice family wedding in a marquee, where everyone knows and likes one another. Dads are dancing embarrassingly with their daughters, friendly in - jokes are being guffawed over and, at the stroke of midnight, everyone sings 'Auld Lang Syne' with gusto and a tangible sense of togetherness. Even difficult - to - cater - for teenagers seem happy and integrated, with a temporary skating rink brought in, fussball tables, air hockey and a computer games room set up for them to flop around in.

The party is a winter version of the Lower Mill Summer Festival a few months previously. Then, on a balmy summer's night, almost the same group of people had gathered for a hog roast, barn dance and quiz, at which the prizes were presented by Darcey Bussell, recently retired as principal ballerina with the Royal Ballet, who happened to be staying with friends on the estate. The wines were good, the picnic food tasteful, the conversation ranged from City deals to sailing to theatre, and the Lower Mill children were, as ever, immaculately behaved and sociable in a way that isn't seen a lot today. Even the ubiquitous dogs at Lower Mill are noticeably good humoured and easy - going. It's as if there's some kind of magic in the air that neutralises aggression of all kinds.

What we are seeing, indeed, is the quintessentially English summer village event - with a significant difference; there can scarcely be a 'real' village in Britain where such a festival would actually happen, let alone in such an atmosphere of classless, good mannered bonhomie. As you watch the residents sitting in groups on picnic rugs drinking, eating and chatting, you are forcibly struck by the fact that, in barely 12 years, an entirely new, wholly self

- propelled community of well - to - do (but not remotely flashy) vacationers has emerged that no longer - and never really did - need Paxton as 'ringmaster'.

The neglected, yet potentially gorgeous, stretch of Cotswolds countryside where he once spotted some enticing - looking lakes from his helicopter and landed for a swim and a snooze is now a fully - fledged community, a residential nature reserve, as he likes to call it - a communal country estate, a pioneering, architecturally and socially adventurous village for the 21st century, with a distinctive buzz and civic spirit.

This tangible sense of community is one of the most remarkable things about Lower Mill. Despite being intensely futuristic, and in a sense an artificial construct, the community also succeeds in being a throwback to a gentler, jollier and, in a multitude of ways, more authentic age - a time when you could leave your bicycle unlocked anywhere (as everyone does on the estate) and not have even the remotest fear that it will have been stolen or tampered with when you return to it.

The Lower Mill Summer Festival had come at the end of a month when a lot of British people were beginning to wonder if Britain was not changing irrevocably for the worse and becoming a worryingly alien place. There had been a spate of street shootings by children across the country; the weather was weird; there had been news days earlier that record numbers of people were emigrating from the UK.

Lower Mill and the Festival may have been a mere blip of time in a hidden away spot on the map, yet it demonstrated vividly that the kind, civilised, quirky, good - hearted Britain we bought into as children, the Britain of Enid Blyton and Arthur Ransome books, may not be entirely a myth, given the right circumstances, British people still are what they were, and have also improved by some measure in the sense of being more tolerant, more liberated and more liberal.

It was fascinating, for example, to see the way Lower Mill dads play an active and equal part in looking after children. At a village fête 50 years ago, a typical middle - class dad would have been a distant figure in a suit and tie, smoking a pipe and looking on with a mixture of bafflement and vague disapproval. Today, he is a young - looking dude in fashionable shorts and a T - shirt, wraparound shades and the baby in his arms. And Lower Mill is his ideal holiday habitat. This isn't just a Lower Mill phenomenon, of course, but it is starkly manifest here, and many people visiting Lower Mill come away thinking of it as something of a template for the way the future will be - not the silly, comic book future of flying cars and Lurex spacesuits future, but the real 21st -century British future.

Another odd thing; there's no question that Lower Mill is overwhelmingly middle class. Yet Lower Mill people are not all mega - rich or metropolitan; there are as many Birmingham and Bristol accents here as there are Kensington. But they're all somehow indefinably *nice* - considerate, concerned modern people.

It all adds up to an adept feat of social engineering on Paxton's part, yet, as he hastens to explain, he didn't really need to engineer anything - he enabled what's happened here, but the growth of community has been quite organic.

'The overwhelming asset here is really good manners,' he says. 'That's because these are hardworking families, and hardworking families were always the backbone of England. And hardworking families exist in all classes, so it's not inconceivable that hardworking, local working - class families could buy a house here. At this stage, one guy has - a fireman who's bought himself a vacation house. How's he done it? Through bloody hard work.'

'The essential element here is that it's a community of likeminded people. You bump into people who are most probably going to be rather like yourself, who you know you

Bourne Ultimatum producer Paul Sandberg takes a break from filming and relaxes at Lower Mill.

Lower Mill Country Club in summer.

Beaver Brunch.

can get on with. Sure, if you want to dip into village life you can walk into villages, and use the pubs and restaurants, which everyone does.'

'But if you actually live in a village, especially as a second home, you won't easily have any of the elements of what country weekends are about. You will have through traffic, rather than be able to walk or cycle to a £5m spa that's yours, or to use an equestrian like the one we have planned. You won't have high quality trout, other game and course fishing, or have any of the vast range of amenities we already have here, and that are growing in scope every year. Here, you have a place to find peace and quiet, to relax, to use the spa, to unwind and to live as a family even if you are divorced, as quite a few of our people are.'

It's one thing, of course, for Paxton to enthuse about the vibrant community that Lower Mill has become, but when homeowners on the estate start to reflect similar - and often more trenchant views - it is, perhaps time to recognise that a powerful phenomenon has emerged in this corner of the Cotswolds.

Mike McKeown, a business development manager for IT giant Cisco, was brought up in villages in Devon and Cornwall and is consequently no stranger to village life. He has a home on Lower Mill with his wife, Annie, and their boys aged seven, ten and 13. 'What's different about it from a normal, home community? I think it's the positive atmosphere,' he says. 'There's a relaxed, friendly, away - from - things mindset. People are more outgoing and generally happier than in everyday life and work. People repeatedly find that in two or three years they make more friends than they do at home in a much longer time. People will often say down here how they've lived in their primary home for ten years and don't even know the name of the person next door. The community has taken time - nine years or more - to develop, but the idea of coming down and meeting friends who are different from your normal work and home friends has become a great attraction.

'It's a safe place to be,' he continues. 'You don't have to worry about traffic or security. A lot of the people from the cities are very security conscious. So for the first six months, they'll carefully lock the doors and then suddenly they realise they don't have, to. They can happily let the kids out for hours and not worry about some nutcase chasing them or trying to sell them drugs.'

'It's very similar to the villages in which I was brought up in that you could just amble down to friends' houses, knock on their door and spend hours outside on a sunny Sunday afternoon mucking about with your mates without having to be ferried around by your parents. The difference at

Lower Mill is that your friends aren't, as they would be in a village, your school friends as well. Here, the friendships building up are based purely on the fact that they happen to live temporarily here at the weekends and holidays. So my kids meet a much broader set of friends.'

Another very typical family of Lower Mill homeowners consists of Andrew Lamb, a commercial property consultant from Bourneville, Birmingham, his wife, Anne, a lawyer, and their boys aged eight and 11. 'The problem with second homes, as we discovered from talking to people, is this thing where your neighbours hate you,' observes Andrew.

'I'd rather buy a mobile home than have that. As a kid, we went caravanning. You'd stop somewhere and within 15 minutes, you'd make friends with the people in the next caravan and your parents were being invited round for a barbecue. It was extremely friendly. It's very, very similar at Lower Mill. The key thing is that everyone's here for fun. So if your neighbours are in, you'll always be in and out for coffee or lunch or a drink in the evening. It's very sociable and definitely not somewhere for privacy.'

'My kids don't stop all day. From the early morning, they're playing football, rugby, outside, discovering. Last night my eldest went with the warden doing a dusk animal watch, looking out for badgers, beavers, water voles, barn owls and so on, with night vision binoculars. My son was reeling off all these things he'd seen and the enthusiasm was absolutely amazing. The whole thing is just so much better and healthier on any number of levels than both "normal" life and "normal" holidays that I really could go on about it for hours.

'But it's not just that it's a place for kids. There's a brilliant adult community, too. Our neighbours, for instance, are a head of commercial property, a lawyer from Bristol, a barrister from London with his wife who's also a lawyer, two medical consultants, and a chairman of a plc. So it's real mixture, a lot of City professionals and entrepreneurs, and the point of my saying all this is not to show off what a professional lot they all are, but to say that nobody I've met so far, not one person, have I thought, "Oh, what an idiot".

'Everybody's very different, obviously, but they're all just very pleasant, polite and open. Since we've been, I've not met a single person who has airs and graces or is stuck up their own bum. It's a mixture of middle - belt England types in terms of what everyone's done, but you can guarantee they're all well educated and, most of all, they're all people who've made their own money. There's no one who seems to have inherited wedge or inherited the business. I find that really interesting.'

The emergence of the community at Lower Mill has similarly turned the head of one of Britain's most respected commentators on property matters, Kevin McCloud, best known for Channel 4's *Grand Designs* and his contentious property column in the *Sunday Times,* in which he takes on planners, architects and developers. Apart from championing architecture and, especially, sustainable construction and urban regeneration, McCloud also campaigns on wildlife issues.

'The great thing about Lower Mill conceptually is that it offers the chance to buy into somewhere people can escape to *in* the UK,' McCloud argues. 'What are the options? Centre Parcs? Buy a caravan? Butlins? Other than that, you're into buying a second home, which has damaging economic effects on local communities. So, in my view, Lower Mill represents a real culture change. It's a classic example of thinking out of the box. We've spent a couple of weekends here and I'm a great fan of it as a family location. We take boats out on the lake and cycle and we have a really good time.'

'If you live in a city, especially, it's a fantastic alternative. It also means, whether you call it ghetto - isation or neighbourhood, the chance to find yourself among like - minded people with the same values, who are interested in the same kind of things, whether that's the broad issues of sustainability or just chilling out and fishing. And those are likely to be the people whose children you want your children to play with. Lower Mill is somewhere where you can chuck your kids out on their bikes for four hours and you don't have to worry about their safety. And that's something very, very valuable.'

'So' he continues, 'isn't that elitist? Maybe, but I say the point is why not bring together people of like minds, why not bring together people who think and enjoy each others' company? So what? Maybe there is an argument that it's elitist, but if you look at the figures compared with the Costa del Sol, the property here is actually at a very good price - plus you have it all the year round.'

'For anyone wanting to build a model community,' McCloud concludes, 'Lower Mill would be the place to look. As you walk around, it's quite apparent that this is a real community based on architecture and landscaping. Architecturally it takes 200 years to make a place and Paxton's managed this in fewer than 20. It does that clever thing of making you feel good, and that's achieved by a combination of the architecture and the planning and the spa. To come somewhere and feel you're being treated to experiences that offer a sharp, simple contrast to everyday life, to create from zero the tremendous sense of peace and quality that you have down here is a clever trick to have pulled off.'

At Lower Mill, catching a 5lb trout triumphs over Xbox.

Even the local authority in nearby Cirencester, which might be expected to look a little askance at least at a development such as Lower Mill, is exceedingly positive about it, not only from an architectural point of view - but looking at the community aspect as well.

Bob Austin, chief executive of Cotswold District Council, explains that most second homes are, naturally enough, in the most attractive, rural chocolate boxy locations. 'We have some villages where 50 per cent of the dwellings are second homes,' Austin explains. 'That has impact. Village pubs, shops, post offices and schools have closed. People coming down here additionally tend to bring with them the sort of lifestyle they have in London. That means inviting friends round for meals rather than going out to a pub. People have hampers of food delivered. A lot never get to know their neighbours; how often, after all, do people in London bump into their neighbour and have a good chat?'

'So the reality is that the second homers entertain in their homes and I suspect the people they're likely to invite round are other second homers who come from a similar background, share similar social mores and so on. I don't think they actively avoid local people but these are, in effect, expat communities very similar in several crucial respects to the kind that form everywhere that people of every culture and nationality go to live abroad.'

'It is well established that people moving into second homes in these quite isolated villages - and we have 300 villages with fewer than 200 people in our area - can and do unbalance the demography dramatically. The houses they buy tend to be small cottages that they knock together. They are the very houses that would once have been two homes for local young married people. I, personally, and the council don't object to second homers. They bring money into the area and we certainly don't discourage that. But the thought is emerging that indigenous populations are becoming outsiders. Lower Mill isn't an isolated community, but it and others in the Cotswold Water Park do mean people of like minds can be together and still enjoy the local area, but in their own, very close environment, where they can be amongst themselves.'

Where, then, is the new Lower Mill community heading? Ultimately, there will be second, third, fourth and subsequent generation Lower Mill owners, just as there are in a traditional village. What will the place be like beyond Paxton's time? How will the community look and feel when the construction has come to an end, the trees are growing and the estate begins to develop, as it inevitably will, a sophisticated patina of beauty and age?

'The main task as we begin to morph from a development into an established place is to continue creating an ever stronger sense of community with societies, clubs and fêtes,' says Paxton says. 'There is already an arts society, a second nature club for children and adults, classes on vegetable growing, charcoal making, wildlife and so on. There's the annual fête with fly - casting competitions, a vegetable growing competition, a football team and a soon to - be - formed wine club with a £1m wine cellar.'

'What I definitely don't want to have is a great big central building that contains everything. The spa is going to be in the first building in what we are calling a farmyard because it will look as though someone has taken a group of farm buildings and tweaked them around and made them modern and contemporary, but fused with the vernacular. It's a big cowshed type building that houses our spa, but then a smaller building will house our wine cellar and another building will be the village hall, because I like the concept of village halls where you have bridge clubs and cookery classes, art and yoga, which can be residential if, say, you've got someone particularly interesting to come and teach cooking and they may be there for a week.'

'The Lower Mill spa is going to be part of a much larger park that will be developed with open air theatre, a sculpture garden and be a social and arts hub, all substantially powered by renewable energy sources. It will be a modern reinterpretation of the village green just as the spa has become the equivalent of a village hall.'

'There will be a second tranquillity spa for adults only, centred on nature. All the treatment rooms will look inwards to a water garden that will support perhaps 3,000 species of wildlife. Somewhere nearby, but sited so as not to disturb residents, there will be a helipad that allows London to be 20 minutes away, although it's only 90 minutes by car and 75 or so by train. Only landings that have been carbon offset will be permitted though.'

'There will be plenty of arts going on, too. There will be a photography workshop for the community, run by a major professional photographer who will have his own studio here. There will be studios for major artists to work from. We also want to create a sense of street somewhere, taking Port Grimaud as a model. So we're planning a street of proper, specialist shops, a Saturday market, a baker and so on. I'm also very keen to build a pub - not a bar, but a proper old boozer with a darts team and a dominos team, but also a Michelin star and a wine list with really fine wines at a decent price.'

'I see us ultimately creating employment in exactly the way that the traditional estates did, with craftsmen working for the estate's established building company, ecologists employed in the field and retailers of natural products working within the estate's mill and shop. When you can gather together 2,000 people who are all ABs and want quirky unusual products, my job increasingly consists of going and searching out things they can't buy - wines that aren't readily available even if they're £500 a bottle, food products they don't see, treatments they can't get elsewhere.'

*"It is all very well buying your manor House, spending hundreds of thousands on restructuring and battling with local authorities to change a lightbulb, but sometimes all you want is a property which affords very little bother for a huge amount of pleasure"*
**Country Life**

*"An exclusive eco-estate is making an architectural splash"*
**Sunday Times**

*"...Will soon have a London Standard restaurant on site - and even has its own organic farm on which residents and their children will be welcome to work for fun"*
**Financial Times**

*"Lower Mill Estate is part nature reserve and part gallery for cutting edge architecture"*
**Country House**

*"It's a beautiful site and houses are well-designed"*
**The Independent**

*"The idea behind Lower Mill Estate is to live surrounded by nature. The nature and wildlife were there first, so they fit the houses around them, not the other way round. Nature comes first, houses second"*
**The Observer**

*"The cacophony of the natural sounds on Lower Mill is completely captivating"*
**Financial Times**

*"Lower Mill Estate in Gloucestershire where sustainable construction, ecology and design come together in one feel-good eco-cuddle"*
**Kevin McCloud**
**Sunday Times**

# 4

## The Orchid

World-renowned nature reserve ... pioneering vacation community of the future ... communal country estate ... beacon of sustainable development - the list of Lower Mill's achievements seems to be added to every year. The development already has an enviable track record for breaking a variety of moulds.

But establishing at the same time a world - leading modernist architectural showcase - the largest collection of modernism in England on one property, no less - is surely an ambition too far for a purpose - built holiday village in the Cotswolds? This is, after all, not just one of the most traditionally rural parts of England, but is almost literally the backyard of the Prince of Wales, the archenemy of modernism.

Not so, it seems. Lower Mill is already in the big time of modern architecture. When news broke in 2008 that work was starting here on one of the most *avant garde* private homes in the world - the extraordinary Orchid

House designed by the young London architect Sarah Featherstone and sold off - plan for over £7m - it only cemented the growing buzz that, along with all its other star qualities, Lower Mill Estate was going to be a global leader in architecture.

Featherstone's wholly asymmetric, pod - like design made headlines around the world and put Lower Mill - which was at the time possibly more famous for its beavers than anything else - firmly on the broadest public radar as an architectural phenomenon. The idea came to Featherstone while she was doodling, inspired by botanical cross sections of the Bee Orchid, which abounds around the site where the house is being built and camouflages itself as a bee. The house will be set in an acre of private woodland and include an earth - roofed artist's studio, a spa and a glass - sided badger set. The site is also a renowned songbird and newt habitat; there are some 30 breeding pairs of nightingales in the surrounding hedge.

Suggest to Bob Austin, chief executive of Cotswold District Council, which gave the Orchid House the official planning go - ahead, that this is an amazing thing to have happened in a part of deepest rural England where the biggest town, Cirencester, has a population of just 22,000, and he affects to be quite surprised - even it is plain he's deeply proud of his authority's leading role in Lower Mill's iconoclasm - in

- action.

'As soon as people hear the name Cotswold District Council, they assume we're pretty restrictive,' Austin says. 'We are 75 per cent Area of Outstanding Natural Beauty, we have 147 conservation areas and 6,000 listed buildings. So it is not where you'd expect the innovative edge of the architectural world would think of to come and put up some really interesting buildings. But the Orchid was one of eight designs put to us by Lower Mill, and we've given planning permission to all of them. There have obviously been sceptics on the planning committee, but this authority has been very comfortable with placing itself at the leading edge of modernist architecture.'

And Lower Mill's place at that leading edge has attracted extravagant praise from some of the most significant names in architecture. Dr Sunand Prasad, president of the Royal Institute of British Architects, speaking of Sarah Featherstone's Orchid House, says: 'Aesthetically, it looks absolutely beautiful and I celebrate it. The British countryside has virtually no modern buildings in it, and now we are going to have this - one of the most interesting and extraordinary country houses to be built anywhere.'

'It's been a long time since something as intriguing and gorgeous looking as this came through and got built, especially in the countryside,' Dr Prasad continues. 'The design is extraordinary. If it has a zero carbon footprint then it sets a trend for the future. It shows that the wealthy aren't there just conspicuously consuming but actually taking things more seriously. And it's such a relief, a joy, that someone can get planning permission for something as adventurous as this.'

Professor Will Alsop, one of the world's leading architects and one whose own outstandingly modern designs for Lower Mill have also received planning permission - comments: 'It's exceptionally beautiful. It will be amongst the most avant garde homes in Europe and possibly the world. There are extraordinary houses in the countryside, but they're rare and not so obviously *avant garde* as Sarah's.'

Professor Alsop, winner of the RIBA Stirling Prize for designing London's Peckham Library, explains: 'What's surprising about it is that it's been given permission and is actually being built now. And it's doubly amazing that in Gloucestershire, which you would expect to be one of our more conservative counties, one can build things like this. One of the problems architects have with projects of this ilk is that the question is asked, "Why hasn't this been done before?" Overseas, that question doesn't count, but here it's regarded as important. So Sarah's Orchid House going ahead opens up a major opportunity and will help do things like this in other parts of the country.'

And the great champion and observer of the built environment, actor - turned - academic Griff Rhys Jones sees Lower Mill as no less than a legacy to the future. 'It's fascinating as architecture and it proves that people react to that by coming and buying,' he says. 'I love the environment. It's like an American vision in a way. I think Lower Mill is something that will be visited in hundreds of years time because it has integrity and a reflection of the age we live in and I admire that.'

'We have to create places where people want to be, which Lower Mill manifestly is. But it also fulfils another of the most important things in architecture, which is a feeling of experiment. I think essentially it's an ecological experiment with houses attached. You have to want to subscribe to that view of the world in order to go there and join in. Yes, it is one man's vision and imagination, one man's dream. But it's no coincidence that the great model towns - the Adams new town in Edinburgh, for instance - were created in the same way, rather than by committee of some sort. So what I admire most about what Paxton is doing is that he is backing his beliefs and creating a space that's a quite dense architectural living space, but in an environment which is developed very sensitively and extremely sound ecologically.'

nd Design's Kevin McCloud chills in the Lower Mill eco pool.

th Allen (Lily's dad) relaxes by pool at Lower Mill.

lywood photographer Jasin Boland bought his wife the ultimate Valentine's gift - a Lower l house and Lower Mill wrapped it for them.

Of all the subjects that enthuse Jeremy Paxton - from nature to sustainability to sports to flying - there's a sense that architecture, and especially what he calls 'the architecture of leisure', is his greatest motivating passion. It is clear that seeing the ever more remarkable homes of Lower Mill rising up in Cotswold stone, steel, glass and interesting angles from the lakes he spotted from the air all those years ago inspires him at every level.

'The underlying impetus at Lower Mill has never been to throw up something inhabitable and cash in,' he says. 'As a team of many, many talents, with everything we have undertaken here, ecology, community, architecture, we've not just gone, "OK, this is the project". We've said, "This is the start. This initiative starts here".

'This is the architecture of leisure, the art of building in a feeling of relaxation and sociability. A place where the design enables you to spend a whole week travelling round by rowing boat seeing your mates, and all within a safe environment. And that I do see as essentially an art initiative. I think the houses by the Lower Mill guys are no less than sculpture in the countryside. It's uplifting. I don't like doing things in a corporate way. Everybody's got to make their money, but I don't want to just recruit some artists to lend respectability. I actually want to regard it as an art project more than a property development. Plus

the ethical process must always underpin and run the
operation.

Everything is committed to renewable technologies. It's
got to be zero net energy.'

'Of course it's the case that some people won't necessarily
appreciate it or even get it, because it's subjective, as any
art is, and they won't buy, and that's fine. The people who
do buy here love it because it isn't suburban with that hard
- edged, manicured look; they can't go and find that in
suburbia. This is their antidote to suburbia. It's also their
antidote to the tired old paradigm of seeing a traditional
Cotswolds house in *Country Life,* buying it and semi -
regretting it for years, as disadvantage after disadvantage
of village life as a permanent outsider dawns on you.'

'Here they've got a 550 - acre estate with 400 acres of wild
flower meadows, rolling landscape, trees, wildlife, over
3,000 species, and if you look around the properties, the
landscaping is all indigenous native species. We don't clip
lawns to 5 cm; we deliberately allow habitats to emerge
around the houses, with some long meadow grasses, with
paths through them. If you look at the Clearwater scheme,
in the middle of the island, our habitat creation scheme has
otters living closer to any human form than hitherto has
been the case in the entire United Kingdom.'

'So it's anything but suburban, but you only have to look at the architecture to see it's not the obvious architecture of the Cotswolds, and neither should it be, because if you just continually copy what was there before then you don't progress anything, artistically. I do see this as an art initiative, combining organic forms, nature and human beings all working in harmony. And I would love, in the end, for it to be recognised as iconic in architecture and design on artistic terms, on a global stage, as the most significant collection of incredible architecture in one location in the world.'

'Even the spa, although its foundation is with nature, is in the style of a giant cowshed that's been converted into a contemporary gallery. You've got long, wide corridors where art is displayed and it's very much about untreated oaks, untreated slate, whitewash walls, superb lighting, recess areas for canvases.'

If there is a single quality that characterises Lower Mill it is its ability endlessly to evolve ideas that are new, but go far beyond being mere novelties. One such initiative is the estate's new self - build concept, whereby a family purchases a plot of land and then, in co - operation with the estate, develop a unique holiday home on it. Lower Mill will introduce the clients to reliable architects, engineers and other consultants to deliver a one - off house at a fixed price and in a fixed timescale. One such family is currently planning to build the estate's first Hufhaus  - the iconic German homes immortalised in Britain by Grand Designs. 'It all amounts to the closest thing the property world has ever come, really, to bespoke tailoring,' says Paxton.

Did Jeremy Paxton always have this mission to infiltrate modernist architecture *en masse,* and with a pure art ethic, into the English countryside? 'I had a strong interest in design when I bought Lower Mill Estate,' he says. 'I wanted to push people towards modernism and I felt that there was a market for modernism. No one else did, other than Richard Reid - the most represented architect at Lower Mill. And Richard was with me and we convinced Cotswold District Council to allow us something that basically resembled LA meeting the Cotswolds.'

'But I would add that I also fell for the Grade II - listed water mill, which is one of just two survivors of its type on the river Thames, so it's not 100 per cent about modernism to the exclusion of every other type of architecture. But once Somerford Villa, the first landmark home to be built and an unashamedly modern house striding out over the water, was purchased at a shade under two million quid, it was clear to both of us that modernism really was going to work in this environment.'

allows, Amazons and carefree memories.

chid - many say the most exciting Avant Garde home in Britain.

Turning Lower Mill into reality has required working closely from day one with Cotswold District Council, and doing so has been a central tenet of Lower Mill's strategy. 'Without the support of the planning authority, you're simply doomed, you just can't make it happen, it's illegal,' says Paxton. 'Once that was cemented, we were able to pull together a small team of a few exciting architects to produce some truly special buildings. Richard Reid and I felt that there was an opportunity to do up to 40.'

'Richard's a sort of unsung hero of architecture. He's an artist who became a Central St Martin's academic. He was professor of architecture at UCLA, visiting professor at Harvard and the University of Bologna and has taught most of the generation of Piers Gough and people like that. And he also a highly respected architect himself, whose work I admired.'

'Together we came up with a plan to recruit a number of architects. It was a bold idea, I guess, to launch modernism in the rural landscape as a way of keeping our brilliant architects at home. The idea wasn't only to create a series of wonderfully celebrated pieces of architecture at Lower Mill; a central part of it was the idea of not then hiding them away behind tall fences and walls but making them available to be seen and possibly rented out by people.'

'Naturally, it then started to get around the architectural world that we had this initiative and were saying, "It's art time, boys, this is unconstrained, it's a blank canvas, you can do what you like." And before long we had about 50 architects who wanted to be involved with it. They got terribly excited about it, even the absolute greats such as Richard Meier, who sent me a one - line email saying, "When do I start?" These are people who really care about architecture, who are not primarily about making money.'

The desire to do something totally pioneering but with a minimum of gimmickry and a maximum of integrity has pervaded Paxton and Meier's thinking. And, moving into new territory for him, Jeremy started designing alongside Meier. 'I'm very involved in the design process, it's really team painting,' says Paxton. Richard and I pore over every single house together, I'll sketch things, he'll sketch them better, I'll change them, he'll make them even better than that.'

'It's not *quite* the case that I was new to design, of course,' Paxton says. 'My dad was very good at making things and when I was about five we built a four - storey hamster cage lined with steel and made out of champagne crates. We built staircases. And for my fifth Christmas, they bought me a proper carpentry set with real saws that could cut. You probably couldn't do it now, the parents would be sent to prison by the health and safety people. But I built stacks of model aircraft and some fantastic gliders with doped cellulose wings. I'd tow them behind my bike.'

Even in the earliest stages of Lower Mill's ascendancy in the architectural world, the idea was starting to form of cross - pollinating with a world - ranking academic centre of excellence and working together to produce something of significance for the public beyond Lower Mill's idyllic, and perhaps privileged, acres.

'I was rapidly becoming aware,' Paxton recalls, 'that the problem with sustainable architecture is that a lot of it looks unappealing at a variety of levels. People don't really want to live in something that looks as if it's made of Mecanno and they also don't want a 30 - year payback period before the sustainability features of a structure begin to make any kind of financial or, indeed, energy - saving sense.'

'The need is for simple energy - saving devices and simple building systems that look desirable and are attractive to live in. But, of course, the big house builders, the people being relied upon to deliver three million homes by 2020, say the no - carbon, ecologically sensitive, sustainable house simply can't be built, at least, not at a price that the average home - seeker can afford. They are, I suspect, perfectly happy with their standard bland, carbon -

aggressive, design - dead, last - the - lifetime - of - the - mortgage developments masquerading as real homes.'

'Now I was aware that there's a great deal of genius that goes through Cambridge University's School of Architecture, and I wanted to really bring that out. The idea of working with established and credible institutions in new concepts for ecologically led, sustainable architecture seemed the way ahead. And if we could, by doing so, provide a template that could be used by other companies globally, we would really be spreading the benefits of the whole Lower Mill ethic beyond our boundaries and beyond our shores.'

'A landscape architect that I had a great deal of respect for introduced me to her husband, who is a professor of architecture at Cambridge, and he introduced me to the head of sustainable architecture, who in turn introduced me to Griff Rhys Jones, who was spearheading a campaign to raise money for the department.'

'So I am hopeful that one day we will establish, as a result of this initiative, the Lower Mill Cambridge Sustainable Home Competition.' The aim of the competition would be to give the impetus to students and alumni to create a mass - marketable, sustainable home of the future but, crucially, one that is deliverable. The carrot will be that the winning competition design will be built on a plot ready and waiting at Lower Mill. And this prototype will be more than a one - off curiosity. 'The aim is to create a new template for sustainable homes,' says Paxton. 'We want to develop something that will allow us to throw away the template of traditional house - building and show the way forward to national developers.'

The judging panel for the planned competition will include architects of global note, as well as noted thinkers from other disciplines. One of the masterplanners for Bilbao, and head of architecture at the university, Professor Marcial Echenique, would chair the panel, with the artistic input from Antony Gormley and the modernist design perspective from Professor Will Alsop. The proposed panel's sustainability expert would be Professor Koen Steemers, director of the University's Martin Centre for Architectural and Urban Studies. Also on the judging panel would be Griff Rhys Jones, Kevin McCloud - and Paxton, to judge if proposed structures can actually be built.

'The winning design will have to be beautiful,' Paxton insists, 'but always with the caveat, of course, that form without function is vacuous, whilst function without form is mind - numbingly ugly. What you're aiming for, function and form working hand in hand, is incredibly satisfying - not least because sometimes the mix of the two is so smooth, it's barely visible'.

'The competition is of central importance to me and very important to Lower Mill. The thing is, I'm not just interested in money. What I'm principally interested in doing is making a difference. I suppose you get to the stage of your life where you think, "What *am* I going to do with the next chunk of it? What can I develop as an interest now that can stay with me forever?"'

*Published by Lower Mill Books.*

*© Lower Mill Books 2010.*

*ISBN 978-0-9565362-0-4*

*Designed by KGK Creative*